Unanchored

by Sarah Thursday

Cover artwork by Esmeralda Villalobos 2013

Thank you to my family & friends, Aly & Mickie, Esme, The Poetry Lab Crew: Danielle, Nancy, Alex, and Tina, every single person part of Cadence Collective. Thank you, Two-Thousand Thirteen for being such a magical year.

SADIE
GIRL
PRESS

ISBN-13: 978-0692472125
ISBN-10: 0692472126
Copyright ©2013
Sarah Thursday
SadieGirlPress.com
3rd Edition Revised (2015)

Table of Contents

Pale Yellow

This is the one, I decide
The one I will speak to
I must be four years old
stamp says "Aug 78"
I am squatting low in a pool
of dirty water near dark green masses
maybe algae or fungi or moss
it's all gross to me now
the background is thick brush
low hanging wall of green leaves
I am smiling
swishing the inches of water
below me- I am in the shade
lucky me
blonde haired child- little girl
nothing on, save pale yellow shorts
my knees pressing on my bare chest
flat thighs and calves
the kind of smile is
one I had on before the camera
centered my image
I was pleased to be there
fingers on the surface of
the unclean water
my rear hanging above the sandy bottom

It's not going to happen now. I refuse to take
her from this moment. I will not speak to this
one. She is perfect and unsuspecting. She
trusts me as I am looking down at her from
my living room couch. She believes I will allow her
to stay there out of the August heat. With her pale
yellow hair past her shoulders, she has no cavities.
She has not yet lost her baby teeth. She is free in
the stream bed alone in nineteen seventy-eight. I
am not going to be the one to take her away from
her perfect moment in the shade out of summer
heat.

Pack Animals

Groups of teenage
boys laughing
like hyenas
still make me
grit my teeth and
tighten my grip
as the twelve
year old me
crosses her arms
across her chest,
pushes her eyes
down like a
criminal when
my only crime
was passing them
on the sidewalk.
Boys in packs
are hunters, not
friends and a twelve
year old girl can't
fight back, so she
learns to walk fast
and smile like an
apology but not
like an offering.

Earth Colored Hair

You were there in my dream
An angel with earth colored hair
Limbs like rushing rivers
As dark and wild as a forest full of fairies
You were tied up like a fault line
Aching to tremor
To crush the stone walls of your mother
Built like dungeons above the ground
You were an aftershock before the fact
Ancient earth rising
Tearing land from history
Your feet tangled deep
In the roots of your mother
She could no longer bear your enormity
An angel bent on destruction
Destroy the landscape
Destroy your inheritance
You fractured through your tragedy
Like a summoned winter avalanche
I had no sanctuary
From your earthen massacre
I waited to be consumed
By branch and bone and soil
But I woke from my dream
With saddened breath
You, an angel with earth colored hair

Once we were angry youth...

Once we were angry youth
shaved heads and colored hair
When I saw you were tragic
I adhered to you
So many secrets to keep
so much truth to grasp
We made honest promises
and everything we felt
it was sacred
Velvet capes and monkey boots
it was The Cure and L.S.U.
Music sang so many things
we knew them all by heart
We sat against the stereo
volume up high
as if to absorb it
inhale its passion
the truth of it all
was in guitar strings
and piano keys
I was anchored to you
in the hurricane of our youth
We outlasted the storm
and the years became memories
and miles grew between us
You and I got regular haircuts
and wore practical shoes
Always and always
I swore to keep us tied
I'd be that solid girl
who cleaned up after
those natural disasters
But the tides have changed
and it's you who set sail
you pulled up the anchor
and I am untethered

The current and our priorities
the list of things we hold as true
are no longer matched
Faithful wife of twenty years
I am still living alone
mother of teenagers
I am the mother of none
woman of the God
I no longer believe in
I know it was only loyalty
that tied us still
You hardly listen to music
and the song in my heart
is the saddest melody
I release you-though you've been gone
We are no longer angry youth
Will you return on another tide
Will time rise and fall
like the ocean waves
Will the anchors never sink
in the same deep waters
I am drifting out far
I know I can swim
But you were the only one
who knew the beginning and the end
long letters in pen and phone calls
salsa and bookstores at midnight
long drives to nowhere for the sake
of the songs on the stereo
and the promises and the secrets
we have none left to keep

Disconnected

There will be no funeral.
No ritual ceremony to close this story.
I loved you. I did.
I swear it over sacred things.
It's dying. Suffocated and left to starve.
This precious fragile entity is a waif of a memory.
It waits to leave this life,
Hardly holding breath.
I used to feed her. Bring her fruits.
Bring her grains and sustenance.
There will be no funeral.
No condolences. No sympathetic cards.
We will die quietly. You will not visit.
You will not see this as a God sent gift.
You will hold to principles and assumptions.
You will allow time to consume us.
Time will erode what we fail to nourish.
It will die of suffocation.
I am suffocating. I am wilting.
You will walk on by. You will go.
To your priorities. To your well planned life.
I weep and mourn for death.
There will be no funeral.
You pruned this off your burden.
This will not be certified. Just gone.

Brown Eyed Boy (But Not a Boy)

You strode in with shoulders
of a man so much taller,
your eyes held back with the tilt
of your head and chin up.

I tried to see you coming from behind
but I was looking for the wrong boy.
There was this guy—not a boy—not a man
but same brown eyes, same brown curls
(and growing). It was you, undeniably.
Your brows were long and circles
under your eyes were set hard.

I know that posture so well,
I've seen it my mirrors past
and in my angry generation.
But you—not you—not your brown eyes,
I have your face memorized like song,
I have loved every inch of it.

I hoped you'd never be familiar
with clenching fists, scraping skin,
bracing the beat of your heart
to stop it from hemorrhaging,
it will callus thick like cartilage.
Grit your teeth and stare them down
without flinching and unbolt the windows.

I have only seen you as a child,
my hand-holding boy in the back seat.
But here you sit, defiant smile,
refusing to play nice—I'm listening.
You now at sixteen, elbows out
tired of rolling with the tide.

You see none that qualifies, all their
smoke and mirrors don't fool us now.
We are all playing the part of the wizard,
but you're far too old for fairy tales.
I want to sing you to sleep, but you
are not six, you need more than lullabies.

You mapped the exits, found the weak hinges
(eventually, you'll see them everywhere).
I can't offer you shit, except how I get it,
I'll stop holding you to that promise
that you will invent that shrink-ray
and keep yourself a child for me.

How He Is Not My Child

I didn't stay up at the hospital until three a.m. waiting for the doctors to assess the situation. I didn't have to be the one to sign papers for the insurance company, for permission to treat, for release of legal responsibility. I didn't have to field the calls, protect him from his mother, sit next to him for hours under the cold florescent lights of anger. I did not bear the weight of pen on paper to surrender my flesh and blood to the intervention of complete strangers. I am not the parent deciding always how much to force him to wake up early, get up out of bed, and live his life, or how much to let him sleep, let him fail classes, let him learn from his own mistakes like a boy on the verge of adulthood. I didn't watch the labor of sixteen years calling out from rooftops for men in uniforms to pull him down, dress his wounds, search for more weapons.

Excuses

I just called to tell you
Sue's transferring soon
To tell you she'll be gone
I just called because I was hoping
You'd want me to come over
I just called to tell you
I made you a tape of songs
Because I don't like you
And I am so moving on
I just called because
There is a movie I thought you'd like
It's playing Friday night
"Sick and Twisted"- just your type
If you're not busy, of course
I just called to tell you
I got better things to do
Because my hormones are going crazy
And my body is this mass of sweaty tension
I just called because I'm still alone
My best friend's still not speaking to me
And I don't know why
I just called because
You make me forget myself
Your one-sided conversations consume
the air so I no longer have to breath
I just called to tell you
I hate this war
I think we're wrong
To tell you about the irony
I saw on the internet
"Make a pact against violence"
As we drop bombs on Kosovo
No double standard there
I just called to tell you
How drunk I wish I was
I watched Futurama again
Did you laugh at all the things
I imagine you'd be laughing at?

I just called- I know what you must think
Desperate girl- I must confess-
I was wrong about you & I being so right
I know you cannot be all the things I need
And that's okay
I just called because I think
This friend thing is a joke
To tell you I don't want you
Don't want to touch your hands
Or your arms or your neck
I don't want to kiss a man with facial hair
To feel your tongue behind those teeth- I don't
I just called to say hi or hello
Or whatever excuse we use
To tell you about this new band
I heard his voice- makes me horny
To tell you I lied about how much I like yours
It's only an eight-eight and a half at best
I just called because I was hoping
We'd really stay friends
And the time you need is finite
Enough to hang around for
To tell you how I prefer my space
Much better than change
Or laughing all the time or fucking
I prefer not to share or take any unnecessary risks
On a guy who can't ever be serious
Or passionate or vulnerable
I just called to tell you
The checks in the mail
And how I wish I lived in New York
Where people run into people on the street
But we stay in our cars and shop
In grocery stores the size of malls
I just called to ask if you were bored
And wanted some company
I hate your answering machine

Rejoice in My Anger and My Apathy

Tiny creatures are living in my stomach
They are living off the lining, gnawing holes
They returned or were dormant for years
They remind me that I've held back too long
That I need to let more of it go
Pack that box, donate to charity
They burrow deep, clenching tight
They love my body in ways I never will
They are singing choruses in unison
They know my diet, my lack of vegetables
They know how many times I've cried
When coffee cannot cure the ache
They love that, it feeds them
When I hold it in, when I stay awake
They rejoice in my anger and my apathy
They love not when I love and laugh
It dissolves them, it starves them
I do battle with them every single day
I count in to breathe and slow release
I lay my hands and rebuke them
I pray to their gods for forgiveness
Soon they must migrate or move on

The Last And Final Poem To N.L.

I loved you
I admit it two years
Since we last spoke
Your potato chip voice
And bony hands
The way you grouped your fingers
At your mouth
And your big off-center teeth
I loved the way you got into your car
Like a grown up with limbs too long
The way you walked into the grocery store
As awkward as a Muppet's legs
You and your rail thin body
And old man's clothes
I loved your shoes
The blue One Stars
And green Vans
I loved the way you couldn't look me in the eye
The way you never took your hat off in three years
And wore glassed on your tiny head
We were children in our grown up bodies
So we went to parks at midnight
And climbed fences in schoolyards
I loved that you still skated at twenty-two
That you liked stickers and sugary Kool-Aid
I loved that you cut my hair
And painted pictures
I only saw once
That you watched G-Force
And lent me taped episodes
Even more, I loved your music
The ones you loved
You gave me Dinosaur Jr.
And the Wedding Present
You read James Joyce and
Introduced me to Holden Caulfield
(Your secret alias)

Your random letters
And indirect thoughts
I overlooked your snobbery
Your cruel remarks
I hoped to be as good as I saw you
Exclusive and without remorse
I loved the way you resisted me
I loved that you spoke to me for hours
On the telephone
I loved you then
For leaving me without apology
For digging this pit in my heart
For watching with me
The train pass deafening loud
And fingers clenched on the chain fence
You said it made you feel empty
I loved you for those words
For hating my poetry
And ridiculing my insecurities
I loved you
I know you did not understand
You thought me unimaginative
I thought you good and hateful and real
I loved you for the tiny things
Like smelly car fresheners
And emails about diluting ice
But you gave the most unkind cut
Words of detest and spite
You, who loved cartoons and butter tortillas
You did not love me
You repulsed at my weakness
Without remorse or hesitation
You broke clean of me
And I was left with your letters
And musical taste

Left with the emptiness of passing trains
Bootleg copies of foreign films
A heart gouged and affected
Left with these descriptive words
And useless opinions
This is to be your last poem
The last time I love you this way
The last of you haunting me
The last conclusion in these memories
But you knew then what my honesty was
A moment's passing thought
You thought my sentiment cheap
I know now, you were so wrong

I Buried You

I buried you—
when you left
it was supposed to be for good.

I dug your grave,
I mourned you for two years.
Your death was crushing
but I had your funeral.
I said my goodbyes.

It was final,
or so I thought until the mail came.
Your name on the envelope—
it gripped my breath
to see your grave broken.

You were shiny at my door
all flesh and bone,
not decayed.

You watered the dust
and grew flowers
of apologies and regret.
Dead hopes, dead dreams
all singing sun bright.

Who wouldn't be sprung—
Who wouldn't feel
miraculous intervention
and long for faith
in redemption
in divinity.

I buried you.
I dug your grave.

You were never supposed
to be standing
here at my door.

Sharon as Segue

We had a talk after our first real date
I used Sharon's *Gold Cell* as segue
poems of damage and fracture
told like a spy from war.
I needed you to know
enough to understand
enough to get why.
Before I shed my clothes
I had to untie those secrets
to lay them out across our laps.
Feet up on the coffee table
I had to look away as I always do
and tell you
how damaged I was
how broken my heart had been
before I ever saw it coming.
How it wouldn't be personal
how it wouldn't be about you
how I carried this weight all my life
how I didn't know if I could rest it.
You sat stone quiet
arm across my shoulders
you kissed my hair
locking your knees under mine.

Summer Drunk

It's the heat, it reeks of his smell
reminds me of the place under his collar
and edges of his long sleeves.

How the air was too thick for sleeping
how I was constantly intoxicated
with the hum of his voice.

I lay in the green sun reading
his books, breathing his fingerprints
heart beats between text replies

The blue sky kissed my shoulders
and thighs, grass ceilings always
bracing my body from ascension.

How I existed in the space
before you with me and without was
sleepwalking and summer drunk.

The heat hung like a red cloud
on my back and on my heels.
Here, the earth comes back

to this place around the sun
to break my sobriety
again and again.

The Silence of Trains

"You fall in love
 with someone who knows
 the same silence as you"
-Daniel McGinn

I fell in love with the man
who knew the same silence—
the silence of trains up close
in roaring motion, the strength
is deafening, a lulling voice
Its constancy feels like comfort

I loved the man who knew
the silence of city lights
from hill tops at midnight
The stars blushing down
at Los Angeles sprawled out
limbs open wide

The silence of public spaces
after dark, after closing,
after all other souls
are empty from it

 I fell in love with the man
whose tongue filled
with paper and sand,
whose throat I saw dancing,
telling secrets, whose hands—
those hands said things
out loud for the first time

I'd been listening for years
Hear it? The silence, it swallows me

Hostage

At work a colleague says to me, "How are you?
The last time we saw you, you ran out
on dinner. We all wondered where you went,
so we held your mom hostage." He jokes,
all smiling up a storm like I'd have
an explanation for him, like I forgot my oven
was on or left my wallet at home. But
I know I've seen him since that night
at a work meeting somewhere. That was
almost exactly five months ago and
I don't bring those memories to work
with me. I don't put the train-wreck
feeling on the player at school while I
got my authoritative hands on my hips.
So I change the subject. He doesn't
know what an ass he's being. Sometimes
they just don't know.

Lies To Tell My Body

My bones are steel-heavy
as I walk the days with it
Pores on my skin ache
weighted by the iron-core earth
pulling me towards her
Down, she says, lay with me

My eyes can't see clear
turn skull-bound, sinking
pregnant with memory
The fibers in my muscles
weep at their loss of it
motion, forward, direction

The nuclei in my cells pull
and push against-toward
refusing to agree with you
Every day, they keep forgetting
why I can't just dial the number
or drive 23 miles northwest

My arms know the exit-curves
(like the length of your limbs)
my feet know how many steps
(like the edge of your sheets)
I don't need my eyes to guide me
my hands, they know what else

But my heart knows to stay
in my honey-thick atmosphere
Lock the windows and doors
breath it in, long breaths
circulating it, the new oxygen
Lie to my body, if need be until
I don't need to remember why

Present Affirmations

I am almost ready
to be over this
I am almost ready
to see you clear
that you were never really
good enough for me
I am almost ready
to pick up the pieces
I set aside
connect those dots
to pull the curtains open
to rip off the bed sheets
flip all the light switches
call you on your bullshit
see you small
and entirely pathetic
this lost puppy
is finding a new home
so you can keep that
old bitch who returned
I will not be lying
outside your door
I am almost ready
to tell you I'm too busy
I don't have time for
this fucked up game
and I'm tossing out
all the possible scenarios
of your apology
of your seduction
of your returning
I'm done with it
I'm almost ready
I am.

Night Birds

At night, late past
twelve, I hear them.

Loud chirping birds
clear like night sounds

unmuddied by day
droning. They are

unapologetic. Sharp-
shouting, "I am heard!"

No contest for their
platform, no shove-

pushing, first-in-line
claim-staking. They

are joyous bastards.

Viscosity

Viscosity is the
resistance of fluid to
eventual deformation by

shear or tensile stress.
Viscosity is due to
friction of opposing

parcels of fluid at
varied velocities.
Pressure is needed to

overcome the friction between
the layers and keep the
fluid moving.

Viscosity depends on
the size, shape, and
attraction between

particles. For example,
honey has a higher
viscosity than water.

A fluid with no
resistance to stress is
known as ideal or

inviscid fluid. This
explains so much about
my life. Am I honey or

am I inviscid?

Ramble

it didn't come today
        all my thoughts are disconnected
how loud my cat is purring
            I didn't sleep well
I had a crappy day
           I miss all my friends
        for a hundred different reasons
how unclear my future is
        how teaching can be exhausting
I have too much love inside
but I won't give it easy
        there are too many tightropes
          of going too far
        of not going far enough
how I know what I need to do
but can't for the life of me
be the one who does it
        I'm always questioning
          my honesty
when should I fight
when should I let it all go
        I can't stop biting my nails
I can't find a home
in someone else's heart
        we are all compartmentalized
          like a bento box
        all on the same plate
        but always on separate sides
I pulled all my anchors
or cut them or dragged them
either way I'm drifting
        even though I own my house
        and I have a steady job

I'm so damn independent
I want some more dependence
                    or a place to rest my head
                        and hear a heartbeat
that knows what I know
                    that will anchor me

and I can be home.

Song Writer

It so often
starts with music
plucking my heart
strings like a harp

that emotional swell
up like a tide
like a current I can't fight
or don't want to

I just lay back
and surrender, float
along the story sung
by the conductor of my

waiting breath, because
it sinks so much deeper
from the top of my throat
through my inner workings

to my lower central
nervous system, down
to the extent of my toes
and back up my thighs

sound is a gift and song-
sung by voice or guitar
violin or piano keys
I devour it all like a greedy

beast, licking its plate
I have never been
satisfied once, so I
became a poet to sing

in the voice God
gave to all poets, song-
writers without notes
without melody, yes

rhythm still, but music
words-not voice-still
breathe on the page and
inhale deep before the next

line. I am singing.

Unknown Employee

I saw a girl at Target, she was me
at twenty-one years old.
She had my blond hair

and simple black-lined eyes,
a red vest and black band shirt
from Joy Division's Unknown

Pleasures. Iconic jagged white
mountain lines I once
plastered to my purse.

The image is a badge, I know
immediately, she is cool
in the way I was cool

working at Target at twenty-one.
I want to tell her we got bigger
plans, even if you can't see it now,

and that boy, who torments your soul,
is just passing by. I want to tell her
we end up alright, and all that confusion

might not get clear,
but it settles. And all that sadness,
the endless sadness fades away,

but I give her a slight grin
and muster, "I like your shirt."
I don't know how else to say it,

so I pay and leave for home.

Sarah Thursday is a music obsessed, Long Beach poetry advocate, and teacher of 4th and 5th graders. She has been writing poetry since she was very young. While investing in her teaching life, she took time off poetry for about 10 years. Circumstances created opportunity to begin writing again and to connect with the poetry community. Through a workshop called The Poetry Lab, she was inspired to begin a website to feature local Long Beach poets and poetry events, called CadenceCollective.net. She continues to work on writing, reading, advocating, promoting, and even performing poetry. Her full length collection, *All the Tiny Anchors*, is available at SadieGirlPress.com! Find her on SarahThursday.com.

www.ingramcontent.com/pod-product-compliance
Lightning Source LLC
Chambersburg PA
CBHW072057040426
42447CB00012BB/3158